Baby Bobcat
Goes to School

By Merry S. Lewis

Illustrations by Lou Lewis

Picture Rocks Publications
Tucson, Arizona
www.picturerockspublications.com

Illustrations by Lou Lewis: p. 1 *Still a Little Shaky;* p. 3 *Where's Mom?;* p. 5 *A Whole New World;* p. 7 *At Attention;* p. 9 *Three of a Kind;* p. 10 *Always Alert;* p. 12 *Watching the World Go By;* p. 14 *Baths Are for the Birds;* p. 15 *Leave Some for Me;* p. 16 *Will It Bite?;* p. 18 *The Lookout;* p. 21 *See You Later;* p. 22 *All Ears.*

ISBN 978-0-9968419-7-9

Text and illustrations copyright ©2015 Merry S. Lewis

All rights reserved. No part of this publication may be reproduced or transmitted in any form or by any means, electronic or mechanical, including photocopying, recording, or any information storage or retrieval system, without permission in writing from the publisher.

Book design by Cynthia Hannon
CynthiaHannon.com

Baby Bobcat is six weeks old.

He has a brother and a sister.

He can stand. His legs are getting strong. It is time for him to learn to be a bobcat.

Mother Bobcat teaches her babies.

The bobcats get ready for school. "Pay attention bobcats."

Mother Bobcat helps them go up a tree. She says, "You can do it. Climbing trees is fun."

Baby Bobcat does not want to come down. Mother Bobcat says, "Come down, come down."

Every day he gets a drink from the bird bath.

His brother and sister
want a drink, too.

The bobcats see a tortoise.
"Come and play," they say.
But the tortoise keeps on eating.

Baby Bobcat hunts for food. He hides by a prickly pear cactus.

Mother Bobcat says, "It is time to go. Follow me." Baby Bobcat and his brother and sister follow Mother Bobcat.

Baby Bobcat listens to his mother. She is a good teacher.

School is fun for bobcats.

Baby Bobcat
had a good day.

Now he can climb a tree.

Now he can
get a drink.

Now he can play with a tortoise.

Now he can find food.

Now he can listen.

Now the bobcats can do many things together.

For more information on using *Baby Bobcat Goes to School* in classrooms, as well as downloadable worksheets, visit www.picturerockspublishing.com.

Credits

About the author:
MERRY S. LEWIS was a teacher for nearly 40 years. She lives in Tucson, Arizona, and bobcat families often visit her yard.

About the illustrator:
LOU LEWIS loved the desert and started painting in retirement.

www.ingramcontent.com/pod-product-compliance
Lightning Source LLC
Chambersburg PA
CBHW040732150426
42811CB00063B/1582